1888 Football League founded

1890 Goal nets introduced

1891 Law in  per except
when h ¿ a player.
Referee pires and
referee.
Penalty

1893 FA Cup Final moved to Crystal Palace

1904 Fédération Internationale de Football Association
(FIFA) formed – England not involved

1906 England joined FIFA. In English, this means the
International Association Football Federation

1923 FA Cup Final staged at Wembley with a crowd of
200,000

1925 Offside law changed. Now only two defenders
needed to put attacker onside, instead of three

1930 World Cup began

1955 European Cup introduced. First floodlit match

1961 Abolition of the maximum £20 per week wage.
Johnny Haynes became first £100 a week player

1965 Introduction of substitutes in competition matches

1966 England won the World Cup

1979 Trevor Francis became the first player to be
transferred for one million pounds

1981 The 100th FA Cup Final took place between
Tottenham Hotspur and Manchester City

*Football is the largest spectator sport in the world
and many of the professional players who delight
large crowds of supporters probably began their
careers as youngsters kicking a ball about in a park
or playground.*

*This book is for those with a basic interest in
football, who want to develop their skills as a
player, either alone or with friends, and to learn
correctly some of the laws of the game.*

Acknowledgments

The author and publishers wish to thank the following for permission
to use the photographs in this book: pages 13 (top right), 28, 30, 32,
46, 47, 48, 50, 51, Sporting Pictures (UK) Ltd; pages 9, 10, 11, 12, 37,
38, 39, 49, Tim Clark; page 6, Duncan Raban, All-Sport Photographic
Ltd; page 13 (top left) Popperfoto; page 7, Harry Stanton.
Also for their help and co-operation: Sportscene of Loughborough;
Subbuteo Sports Games Ltd; and Leicester City Football Club.
Cover by Hurlston Design Ltd.

First edition

© LADYBIRD BOOKS LTD MCMLXXXII

Football

written by JOHN P BAKER
illustrations by PETER ROBINSON

Ladybird Books Loughborough

A pitch to play on

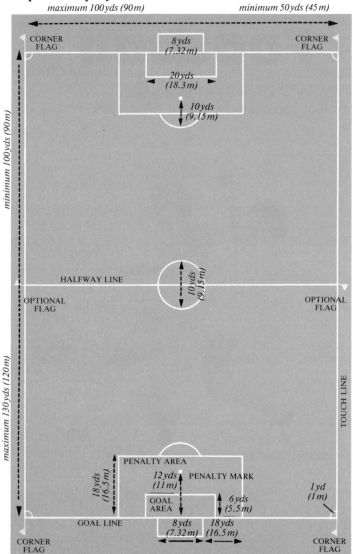

maximum 100 yds (90 m) *minimum 50 yds (45 m)*

CORNER FLAG

CORNER FLAG

8 yds (7.32 m)

20 yds (18.3 m)

10 yds (9.15 m)

minimum 100 yds (90 m)

HALFWAY LINE

10 yds (9.15 m)

OPTIONAL FLAG

OPTIONAL FLAG

maximum 130 yds (120 m)

TOUCH LINE

PENALTY AREA

18 yds (16.5 m)

12 yds (11 m)

PENALTY MARK

GOAL AREA

6 yds (5.5 m)

1 yd (1 m)

GOAL LINE

8 yds (7.32 m)

18 yds (16.5 m)

CORNER FLAG

CORNER FLAG

Metric equivalents as approved by the International Football Association Board

4

This is what a football pitch looks like today but it has not always been like this. After the times when football was played in the streets, between teams from neighbouring villages, a pitch was introduced to limit the game and this pitch was about twice the size of today's grounds – up to 200 yards (180 m) long. You'll notice that pitches can vary in size quite a lot. In fact you could get two small pitches sideways on a maximum sized pitch.

Even though the boundaries of the pitch can vary to suit the size of the field available, the areas within the pitch must always be the regulation sizes. A penalty area, for instance, is always a rectangle measuring 44 yards (39.5 m) by 18 yards (16.5 m) whichever ground you visit. Incidentally the pitch isn't allowed to be square. You may not make the touch line a minimum of 100 yards (90 m) and the goal line a maximum of 100 yards (90 m). The length must always be greater than the width of the pitch.

The goals are obviously very important and must be centrally placed on each goal line. The size of the goals is 8 yards wide (7.32 m) by 8 feet high (2.44 m) but they can be made smaller for young players. Cross-bars replaced tape or rope some time ago to save terrible arguments. If nets are used, they must be' attached to the cross-bar and posts and be pegged down to the ground. It is also important to make sure they don't get in the goalkeeper's way and that they don't have any holes large enough for the ball to get through.

The referee awards an indirect free kick during a match

Most of us think of a referee as the person who controls the match and sees that the game runs smoothly and is played fairly. This is true but he also has a job to do before the game starts.

The referee inspects the pitch and he has to be very careful to make sure that there is nothing dangerous which might cause injury to the players. If the corner flag posts are shorter than 5 feet (1.5 m) there is a chance that players could fall onto them. They have to have a flag at the top, usually the club colours, and the top mustn't be pointed. The two flag posts at the halfway line needn't be there, but if they are used they must be set back one yard from the line so that they don't get in the players' way.

The referee checks the surface of the ground for danger, particularly on wintry days, and makes sure that all the areas are properly marked out.

Small side competitions

One of the problems of playing on a full size pitch with ten other players in your team is that you don't get to play the ball very often. For this reason many schools and teams in training sessions use a five-a-side game to keep players in contact with the play as much as possible. The game is often very fast because it is usually played on an indoor pitch and there are no throw-ins; the ball rebounds into play. The pitch is about half the size of a normal pitch and the goalkeeper's area is a semi-circle of 25 ft (7.5 m) radius with a penalty mark at 20 ft (6 m) from the goal line. The goals are 16 ft (4.8 m) by 4 ft (1.2 m). Different rules can be introduced to help improve skills, for example not allowing the ball to be kicked above head height and restricting the distance from goal that you are allowed to shoot.

A ball to play with

As you walk along the street you may be tempted to kick little objects that lie on the pavements. This is probably how football grew, developing from an individual pastime to involving friends, forming teams and so on. The kicked stone changed to an inflated animal bladder (most often a pig's bladder) which later got a leather case.

Modern footballs are made up of leather panels. Some have 18 panels arranged in six groups of three (see picture left), but with constant blowing up they can lose their shape.

The 32 panel ball (see picture right) stretches less. Footballs should be spherical; if you spin them in your fingers the shape you see should always be round without any bumps sticking out.

A waterproof coating is now used to prevent the ball picking up too much moisture during the game and becoming heavy.

Footballs used to have laces and it was a difficult job to blow them up and do the lace up neatly. You had to be careful not to leave the lace so that it hurt players when they headed the ball. Nowadays, we just see a valve opening and it is very easy to pump a ball up. Referees check that the valve is not going to be a danger to players.

The ball has to be inflated correctly. A size 5 ball is used by adults, and the correct circumference is between 27 and 28 inches (68-71 cm). A referee can usually tell if the ball is at the correct pressure by squeezing it. If you like statistics, the pressure should be 9 to 10.5 lbs per square inch, at sea level.

School teams sometimes use a size 4 ball which is an inch (2.5 cm) smaller. The laws of football also allow women to use the smaller ball.

Footballs nowadays are usually red, white or orange so that they can be seen more clearly. Another ball of the same colour should be used if the first one needs to be changed during a match. Experiments have been tried with different colours to improve visibility.

Some of the footballs currently available, including the official Football League ball (right)

The referee is the person to give permission for a ball to be changed during a game. A nice gesture some clubs make is to present the match ball to a player who scores a 'hat trick' (3 goals) in the match.

Clubs have to have lots of footballs for matches and training. Because balls are very expensive, clubs usually try to find a local firm to sponsor the match ball every week.

Footwear

The laws of Association Football now refer to footwear, not just boots, because the old brown leather boots with high ankles have been replaced by the more modern, lightweight shoe with a moulded sole or screw-in studs.

A leather stud

Studs made of leather, with nails to bang into the sole of the boot, used to be used. The nails had to be filed down as each strip of leather wore away or a player might leave a nasty gash on an opponent's leg.

Nowadays, players are like racing drivers who choose the right tyres to suit the road conditions. Footballers have long studs for soft muddy grounds, short studs or moulded soles for harder pitches, and training shoes, with grooves or suction pads, for bone-dry pitches or icy conditions.

Training shoes

Moulded soles

Longer screw-in studs

Football kit

Recently, manufacturers have persuaded clubs to be more fashion conscious in their choice of kit. Replicas have been produced in smaller sizes and young players now wear football shirts and track suits for more than just football matches. As well as the club badge, the outfit usually carries the trademark of the manufacturer. Some clubs have been able to obtain sponsorship and wear the name of the firm or product on their shirts and track suits.

A sample of some of the kit available in smaller sizes, showing club badges and trademarks

Below: *Vince Hilaire in modern England strip*

Above: *Stanley Matthews, famous England and Blackpool footballer, taken in 1954*

All this is a far cry from the old, long, baggy shorts; heavy cotton, long-sleeved shirts; and thick woollen stockings with shin pads made of strips of cane inside canvas or leather, worn by players in the past.

Not only have the players become more fashion conscious but so have the club supporters. They wear a wide range of hats, scarves and clothing all in their club's colours. Also swopping and collecting match programmes, which are more like club magazines with contributions from members, has become an international hobby.

Things you ought to know about the laws of the game

When you take up a new sport you should try to find out as much as you can about it and learn the rules. This often doesn't happen with football because you pick up knowledge as you play. Unfortunately this causes problems, because the rules passed on by other players are not necessarily the official laws of the game. You may not know that at the time, and bad habits become part of your game. It comes as a bit of a shock when you learn that what you thought was law is just a fairy tale. As a referee, I came across a lot of misunderstandings so I hope that this section will improve your knowledge.

The captain winning the 'toss' has the choice of ends OR he can choose to have the kick-off.

If something or someone (eg dog, spectator), not taking part in the game, stops the ball, the referee must 'drop the ball' (restart the game). If this happens when a penalty kick is being taken, it must be taken again.

If a player accidentally scores an own goal direct from a free kick to his side, it doesn't count as a goal.

If the ball hits the referee, play goes on. If the ball hits the referee and goes out of play, he decides which player played it last and the opposing side restarts the game.

When a referee holds his arm above his head at a free kick, he is signalling that the kick is indirect; *that means that a goal cannot be scored directly from it.*

During a penalty kick the goalkeeper must stay on his line, between the posts, until the ball is kicked. The ball must be kicked forward – not passed back to a colleague.

High kicking is only an offence if it puts another player in danger.

10 yards (9.15 m)

For a corner kick, the whole of the ball must be inside the corner arc. Opponents must be 10 yards (9.15 m) from the ball.

15

Offside

The offside law causes referees a lot of problems because it often means the difference between a goal or no goal. It was introduced in Eton in 1867 to stop 'sneakers' or 'goal hangers' getting behind the defence and waiting just to shoot at goal. It required three defenders, nearer to their own goal line than the player, to keep him onside. In 1925, when goals seemed almost impossible to come by, the law was changed and required only two defenders. In 1978 the law was again re-written but the only change was that players could not be put onside by the ball being played or touched by an opponent.

Some offside problems

People often forget that offside is judged at the moment the ball is played by a team-mate.

When the ball is played by A, team-mate B is clearly onside

As the ball is in the air, defender C moves out and attacker B moves upfield

When attacker B gets the ball he appears to be offside but is not because of his position when the ball was played

REMEMBER:

Offside is judged at the moment the ball is *played* by a team-mate.

The laws of football give the referee the authority to deal with a player who is not playing the ball but is in an offside position. The decision is made if, IN THE OPINION OF THE REFEREE, the player concerned is interfering with play or an opponent, or is seeking to gain an advantage. Any amount of analysis by slow motion television does not alter the fact that the referee is the only judge on the field at the time, and his decision is final.

A player *cannot* be offside if he receives the ball direct from

1 *goal kick*
2 *corner kick*
3 *throw-in*
4 *drop ball*

He *can* be offside if *he receives the ball direct from a free kick* or *when a penalty kick is being taken* if the ball rebounds in that player's favour.

At all restarts, except when the ball is dropped by the referee, the player must not play the ball a second time before it has been played or touched by another player.

At goal kicks and free kicks in the penalty area, the ball must pass outside the area before it is played again. All opponents must be outside the area until the kick is taken.

At an indirect free kick to the attacking team, less than 10yds (9.15m) from the goal, the defenders may stand on the goal line, but only between the posts.

At a throw-in, the player must stand with part of both feet on or behind the line. This means that part of both feet may also be in front of the line.

A goal cannot be scored direct from

goal kick

throw-in

indirect free kick

place kick or kick off

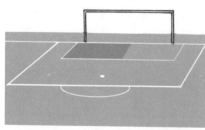

A goal kick or free kick to the defenders in their own goal area may be taken from anywhere in that half of the goal area.

A goalkeeper kicking the ball out of his hands may go outside the area as long as he has first released the ball.

Working towards skills

Fitness

Footballers today have to be very fit because the game is very fast. You should work towards increase in:

Stamina, which will keep you going for 90 minutes.

Speed, for a fast break towards goal, or to recover to help the defence.

Strength, because kicking and heading make running even more tiring.

In your fitness training you have to remember the three 'S's.

Cross country running helps to build your strength and stamina but vary the distance you run and don't just keep to the same pace all the time.

Think about a game; sometimes you are walking, sometimes jogging, sometimes sprinting. Think about this during your training and vary your speeds. Set yourself training targets and try to improve during each session. Try the sequence in the diagram, around a rectangle; a penalty area will do fine.

walk——— jog——— sprint ———

How many circuits can you do and how long does each one take?

During a game you will need to vary your pace; be able to change speed and direction rapidly; have to weave in and out of opposing players and occasionally run backwards.

Set yourself these tasks in training and be prepared to work hard at your weaknesses. Set up some obstacles to run round.

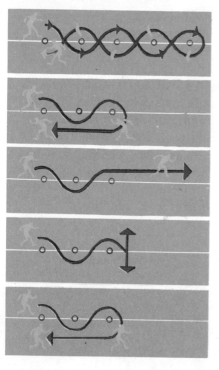

Weave in and out of the objects at speed.

At a certain point *sprint* back for home

. . . or for the end

. . . or to the left or right

. . . or run backwards to the start.

You can add variety and interest by competing against a partner, timing your efforts and trying the tests with a ball at your feet.

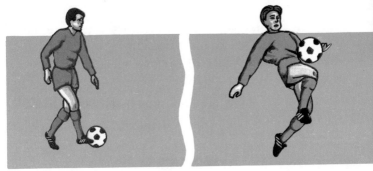

Trapping the ball with feet   *thigh*

Ball control

Being able to bring the ball under control quickly is a very important skill, particularly when you are under pressure from an opponent. Trapping, or 'killing', the ball, to bring it under control, can be done with your feet, thighs, chest or head, but one important rule has to be remembered in all cases; you have to cushion the movement of the ball at the moment it hits you, to stop it rebounding.

PRACTISE THESE SKILLS

Partner throws the ball at different heights

Kick the ball against a wall; take up control and repeat

chest *head*

Imagine the difference between a ball striking a brick wall and the ball that lands in a muddy puddle. You have to aim for somewhere between these two. You need to relax your muscles when the ball strikes you in order to cushion the ball. You must also keep your eyes on the ball but then look up immediately to see what you can do with it next.

Finally, remember that football is a moving game so practise these skills *on the move*.

With a partner 25 yards (23 m) away, hit the ball hard to each other

In a five-a-side game, allow only two touches before the ball is passed

Dribbling and passing

Watching a player running at the defence with the ball at his feet, or a player on the wing, dribbling round a defender and leaving him standing, is very exciting. However if the pass at the end is a poor one then all the effort was for nothing. Dribbling and passing skills go together and need a lot of hard work. Good balance, to sway either way as an opponent approaches and the ability to change pace suddenly, are good skills. Dribbling also needs close control of the ball and the use of both feet. If the ball is pushed too far in front of you, an opponent will soon take possession. Like many of the basic football skills, plenty of hard work using a *tennis* ball is useful.

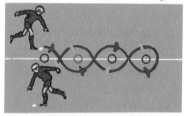

Running in and out of obstacles with the ball at your feet is good practice

In team practice sessions, the other players can be the obstacles if you all have a ball and have to keep within an area

Dribbling relays make the practice more competitive

One of the ways dribbling and passing can be used successfully is to draw an opponent towards you and then pass into the space he has left behind. Or you could use the 'wall' pass:

A dribbles towards his opponent then passes out to B, who puts the ball past the opponent for A to run on to. A is using B as a 'wall', off which to rebound the ball.

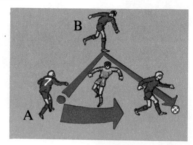

Using a real wall, this time practise kicking the ball and controlling the rebound; dribbling, kicking again, controlling the rebound and so on, along the wall and back. Use both feet as this is good practice.

In close passing situations, it is better to pass to the feet. But if the player is running, try to put the ball just in front of him.

Remember there are times when passing is better than dribbling, for instance, in front of your own goal.

Kicking and shooting

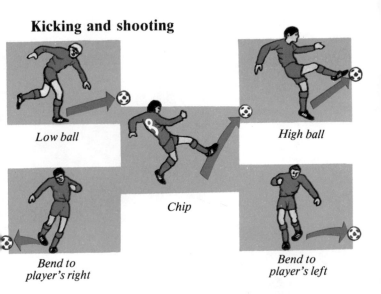

Low ball

Chip

High ball

Bend to player's right

Bend to player's left

It is important to kick with the right part of the boot. The lace part or *instep* will give power and accuracy. The inside and outside edges will swerve or bend the ball. The toe of the boot causes spin and inaccuracy.

Try to get your non-kicking foot alongside the ball, and your body, particularly your head, over the ball, if you want to keep it low. If you lean back the ball will lift. The chip is made by keeping the non-kicking foot behind the ball and leaning back.

In all kicks it is important to get a good backlift and follow through with the kicking foot, just as golfers do with their clubs. When bending a ball, hit it left or right of centre with the inside or outside of the boot, depending on the way you want it to bend.

Involve more players to keep the practice interesting

Shoot at the goal from many different angles

Let a friend tell you which target to aim for

Include defenders in your shooting practice to put pressure on yourself

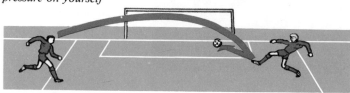

Practise volleys as well as just rolling balls

Heading the ball

This must be done properly or it can be very painful. The middle of the forehead is the correct part to use but you should watch the ball all the time. Power and direction are given by meeting the ball full on, and making use of the muscles at the back of the neck to catapult the head forward and strike the ball.

A good header times his jump so that he is up in the air, has time to swivel his body from the waist, and direct the ball as he wishes. Defenders tend to concentrate on the force of the header while attackers are aiming for a target. If you don't get high enough in your jump, the ball will lift and fly over the cross-bar.

David Hay outjumps Osvaldo Ardilles

Gain in confidence by heading with a balloon or light ball. Learn to guide it

Practise against a wall and keep the score of successful rallies

Include more people. Try to keep the ball up in the air. Concentrate on directing the ball to the other players

Jump and dive to get to the height of the ball

Head tennis is a good game for practice

Tackling for the ball

Possession is important in football and so if your opponent has the ball, you've got to get it from him. Determination to get the ball is a good quality because half-hearted tackles win nothing, except injuries.

Determination to win the ball is important

The sliding tackle can be effective but if your opponent beats you, you will not be able to recover quickly

Tips for tacklers

Keep your eyes on the ball.

Watch for any sway or swerve to 'sell you a dummy'.

Be aware of other players your opponent may pass to.

Keep pressure on your man by staying as close as you can.

Watch for the best moment to tackle; perhaps when he's off balance.

Tackle from in front or from the side, never from behind.

Don't give away a free kick with dangerous tackles.

If you are beaten, recover quickly and have another try.

Two or three-a-side games with only a skittle to aim at give plenty of dribbling and tackling practice. You must beat a man before you can pass, might be a rule worth adding.

Work out dribble and tackle routines with a partner.

In team practice the defenders could all face the same way, around a circle, and the attackers take on one after another. It's important to change around because all players need all skills.

Goalkeeping is a very special skill. You can save your team from defeat and give sufficient confidence to the players in front of you so that they also do well.

Some of the good qualities of goalkeepers

Confidence — to come out when necessary and know you can get the ball.

Courage — to dive at the feet of someone rushing towards goal.

Concentration — when you may not be involved for a long period.

Quick reaction — because you won't get second chances.

Agility — to cover a goal which is about 32 times as big as you are.

Make sure of safety. Get as much of your body behind the ball as possible. Keep your eyes on the ball.

For low balls, get down to them; keep your legs closed and watch that the ball doesn't 'bobble' on the uneven pitch.

When goalkeepers stop the ball with their feet it isn't just luck. They spread themselves as much as possible.

It takes a brave goalkeeper to dive at a forward's feet and smother the ball.

Catching the ball

Above head height
Take off on the move. Keep your eyes on the ball. Get as high as you can. Use both hands

Chest or head height
Jump to cradle the ball comfortably and safely into your body

To your left or right
Try to get both hands to the ball. Hold on tight. Bring it into the safety of your body quickly

Dealing with high centres

Tipping over the bar
With the dropping ball or high centre it may be safer to tip it over the bar

Punching
If you are under pressure punch the ball hard with both fists

Catching
It is safer to catch the ball whenever possible

Narrowing the area to shoot at

If a goalkeeper stays on his line, the attacker can easily place the ball out of reach to either side (diagram 1).

As the goalkeeper advances he puts the player under pressure and can cover more of his goal with a dive to his left or right (diagram 2).

Getting the game going again

Kicking
Practise using alternate feet. Think before kicking. Don't give the ball away

Throwing
This can be quicker and more accurate

Underarm throw
Rolling the ball out to a nearby defender or midfield man can set up a move quickly

Developing different styles of play

It is very important to practise and improve your individual skills but don't forget that football is a team game. We all get very cross with the greedy player who keeps the ball to himself when a good pass would have opened up a lot of possibilities.

The early game of football was concerned with one man getting the ball and dribbling towards goal on his own. The Scottish International Team, in Victorian times, taught us the value of team work.

In the modern game, a tremendous amount of hard work is done by midfield players who run miles during a game. They can read the game and, by anticipating the movement of the ball and the players, they turn up in the right place at the right time to make a vital pass or interception to foil an attack.

Remember to run into space to make yourself available for a pass.

When you are playing the ball yourself, keep looking around to see where the other players, of both sides, are.

Over the years the formations in which teams play have changed as you can see from the football game pictures on the following pages.

What do you think are the advantages and disadvantages of each different formation?

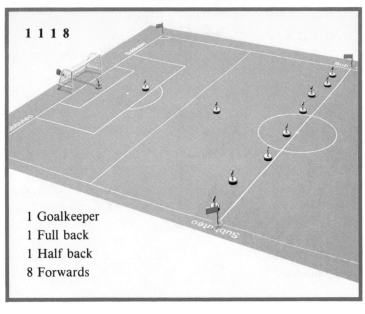

1 1 1 8

1 Goalkeeper
1 Full back
1 Half back
8 Forwards

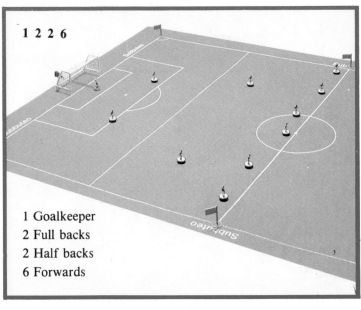

1 2 2 6

1 Goalkeeper
2 Full backs
2 Half backs
6 Forwards

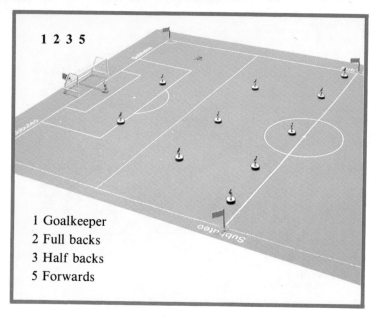

1 2 3 5

1 Goalkeeper
2 Full backs
3 Half backs
5 Forwards

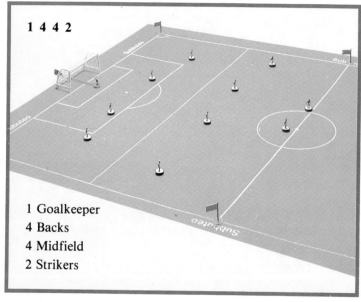

1 4 4 2

1 Goalkeeper
4 Backs
4 Midfield
2 Strikers

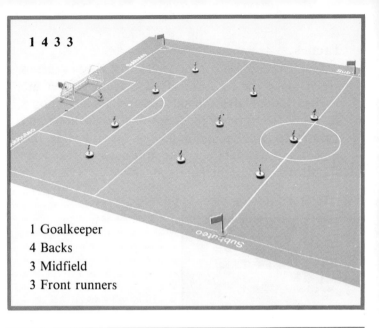

1 4 3 3

1 Goalkeeper
4 Backs
3 Midfield
3 Front runners

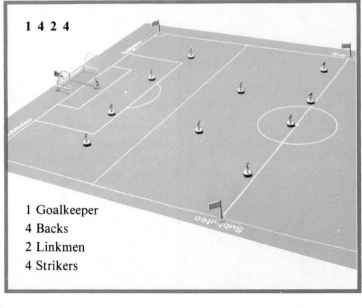

1 4 2 4

1 Goalkeeper
4 Backs
2 Linkmen
4 Strikers

Tactics

Teams today are coached very carefully in tactics which make the best use of all players. Moves are worked out involving many players. Passing moves are preferred to the big kick up-field in the hope that team-mates will get the ball. Try the following five approaches to goal. Vary the approach so that your opponents can't anticipate your moves.

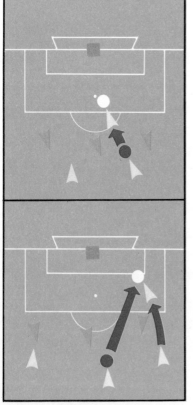

It is very exciting to see a player run at the defence with the ball at his feet.

Try splitting the defence with a carefully directed pass for the front men to run on to. This is particularly successful if your opponents are playing the offside trap (see page 16).

Full backs are used
as wing men, running
forward, overlapping
the midfield, and
putting good crosses
over for the front
runners.

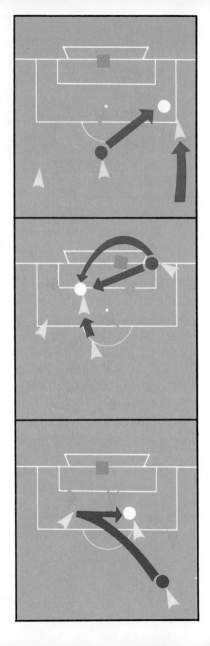

A ball taken to the
goal line and then cut
back into the penalty
area gives an
opportunity for
strikers to run on and
shoot. Try high and
low crosses.

Tall strikers make
good target men for
high crosses. They
can head towards goal
or knock the ball
down for a colleague
to run on to.

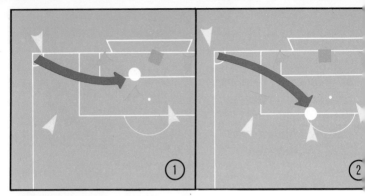

Set pieces – *Corner kicks*

Teams have the opportunity to prepare set pieces. Variety again is important to surprise the defence. The cross should be sufficiently far out to make the goalkeeper think twice about coming out and to give the strikers a chance to run in and head on or volley for goal. The inswinger should be hit with the inside left foot to go to the right, or the inside right foot to go to the left (1). For the outswinger (2), use the outside of the foot. The near post corner (3) uses the front man to head on a cross kick, or go for goal. The short corner (4) can use other players to change the direction of the cross, to confuse the defenders.

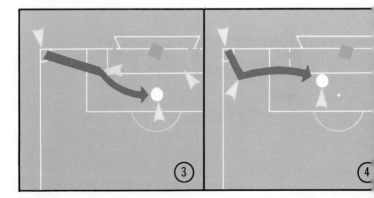

Counter attack

Try to convert defence into attack, quickly. Watch for the opportunity to make a counter attack while the opponents are committed to attack.

Throw-ins

Try to get the ball in play as quickly as possible before the defence reforms. The receiving player should not make himself available too soon, to avoid marking. To the header and back to the thrower, is a useful move.

Long throw-in

This can be as good as a corner, if taken correctly. Make sure you use both hands and keep part of both feet on or behind the touch line.

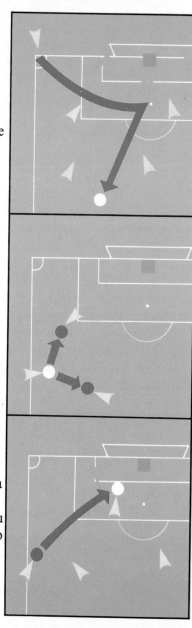

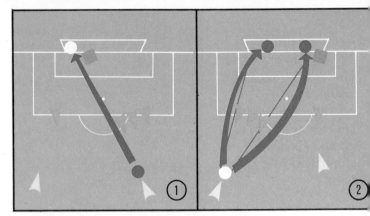

Set pieces – *Free kicks*

The crowd love to see a free kick hit with power and accuracy, to beat the wall and the goalkeeper (1). Alternatively you can rehearse the bending skills on page 26, with the goal as target (2). One method of beating the defensive wall is to pass the ball to a colleague who has a clearer shot at goal (3). Other attackers have an important part to play in acting as decoys (4), to make the defence uncertain about where the ball is going.

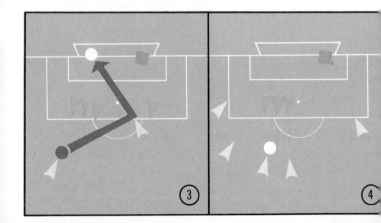

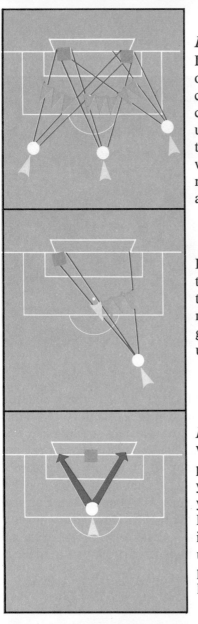

Defensive walls

Let the goalkeeper organise the wall to cover the areas he cannot reach. Don't use more defenders than you need. You will need some to mark the attackers acting as decoys.

Putting attackers in the wall can confuse the defence or even mask the view the goalkeeper had lined up for himself.

Penalty kicks

When you take a penalty kick, make your mind up where you want it to go. Drive it hard just inside one of the goal uprights. The sheer power should beat the keeper.

People involved in the game
Manager and Coach

The manager of a football team is the man who motivates the players and inspires them towards the success they all long for. He has to organise the playing, coaching and scouting staff to get the best out of the club and look to the future. The team's style of play is the manager's choice and this may be influenced by the information he has collected on the opposing team before the match. During the game he will be watching the team's performance and deciding if he needs to change the pattern of play or to make a substitution.

The coach has the job of taking the individual skills of the players and blending them into a team performance. He takes responsibility for the training sessions, keeping the players fit and perfecting their skills. He has to keep the training interesting so that the players enjoy it and don't get bored. During a game he has to assess how things are going and make any adjustments to cover any weaknesses. The set pieces and tactics are worked out in training sessions under the guidance of the coach. He has to work very closely with the manager.

Training session

The trainer and physiotherapist

When a player is injured, we all look to the trainer's bench and expect someone to come and help him to recover. The man who runs on is the club trainer or physiotherapist. He used to carry a sponge in a bladder of water and the crowd would shudder for the player as the cold water was applied. Now the portable medical kit he carries contains smelling salts, pain relieving spray, plasters, antiseptic creams, crepe bandages and many other aids to get the player back into action as quickly as possible. He has to know just what he's doing and is usually a highly qualified person.

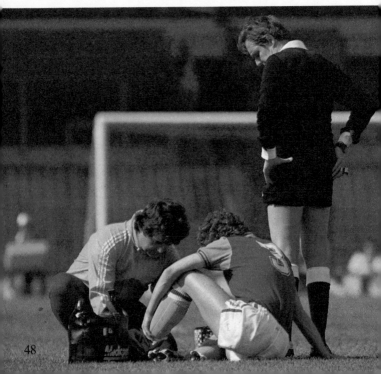

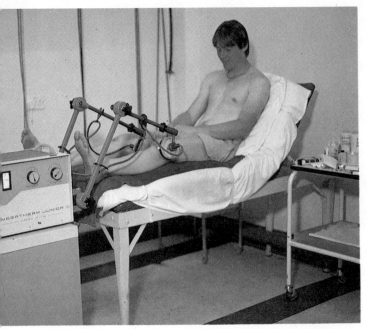

A treatment room with a player receiving heat treatment for a knee injury

At the beginning of the season, and whenever a new player is going to be bought, the physiotherapist will arrange medical examinations and, with the club doctor, will make sure that the playing staff is up to full fitness. During the week he will hold regular sick parades to see which players require treatment. He has a number of facilities in his treatment room including heat treatment for muscles, ultra violet lamps and massage machines. He holds a very responsible position, for none of us wants to see our favourite player out of the team through injury.

Referees and linesmen

Referees and linesmen have important jobs to do and if they do them well, no one knows that they are there. Certain duties concerning the pitch, the ball and equipment have to be performed before the game. On the field the referee has to make sure that the game is played in accordance with the agreed set of laws. He has to award free kicks on occasions when players break these laws and sometimes he has to take further action and caution a player or send him from the field of play. He keeps a record of the game and sees that the correct time is played, making allowances for lost time. He decides if injured players are to be treated on the field or should go to the touch line.

Early in the game's history, matches were controlled by two umpires, one from each team, and the referee was only called on to decide any arguments. He was *referred* to. In 1891 these three officials all became people not connected with the club. The referee became the man in charge and he was assisted by two linesmen who performed outside the boundary lines.

Today, referees and linesmen work together using a set of guide lines which they have worked out in discussion before the game. Linesmen don't make any decisions, they simply draw the referee's attention to things they see and the referee acts as he thinks fit.

The laws of the game are discussed every year by the International Football Association Board. The *Referee's Chart and Player's Guide to the Laws of Association Football* is published after this meeting to set out the laws as they apply for the next season. Every player should study these laws.

INDEX